The Utah-Colorado
MOUNTAIN BIKE TRAIL SYSTEM
Route I - Moab to Loma

KOKOPELLI'S TRAIL
by
Peggy Utesch

EDITED BY F. A. BARNES

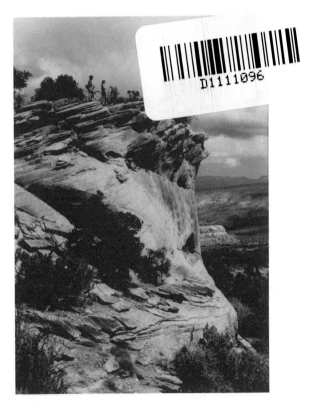

Another Canyon Country Guidebook
1990

1

This book is an illustrated guide to
mountain biking the 130-mile designated route
between Moab, Utah, and Loma, Colorado

It is the 22nd in a series of practical guides to
travel and recreation in the scenic
Canyon Country region of the
Four Corners States.

Text and interior sketches by Peggy Utesch

Photographs as credited

Maps and charts by Bob Utesch

Cover graphics by F. A. Barnes

Chuck Nichols, Nichols Expeditions, Moab, Utah

Copyright 1990 by Canyon Country Publications
P.O. Box 963, Moab, UT 84532

ISBN 0-9614586-9-0
Library of Congress Catalog Number 90-81500

CONTENTS

View from near Mile 9 Segment 3 - F. A. Barnes

INTRODUCTION

This is the first in a planned series of guidebooks describing mountain biking routes in eastern Utah and western Colorado. These routes are being planned and built by the Department of the Interior, Bureau of Land Management, in cooperation with a variety of mountain biking organizations. Our goal is to expand the exciting and challenging sport of mountain biking into areas of canyon country that are not currently known.

The rugged desert terrain of Route I, also known as "Kokopelli's Trail," combines challenging ascents over a variety of trail surfaces, screaming descents for those who dare, and scenery that fuels the soul. With its magical variety and awe-inspiring geologic formations, mountain biking in canyon country is an experience second to none.

In addition to the Moab-Loma Route described here, Canyon Country Publications offers additional guidebooks for exploring southeastern Utah's high-desert terrain. A listing of these publications can be found under "Further Reading."

Travel safely, travel wisely, and respect the desert --

-- and it will reveal its time-held secrets for your enjoyment.

Segment 3 - F. A. Barnes

LOGISTICS

The Moab-Loma Mountain Biking Route (Kokopelli's Trail) is 139 miles of challenging, beautiful high-desert riding. This guidebook divides that distance into six one-day trips that can be ridden one at a time, or combined into multi-day trips. Any of these trips can be accomplished in a number of ways:

Bike Camping: For the hardiest riders, this method is the most rewarding. It can also be the most dangerous. Riding long stretches in the desert requires careful planning and lots of water. Leaving caches of water and food along the trail ahead of time, or having a friend rendezvous to re- supply riders, are two options.

Biking/Car Camping: This enjoyable style of mountain biking the desert allows riders to travel light and cover large distances in a single day. Using two cars, riders can leave a car at the trail end and either camp there at the end of the ride or shuttle back to the trailhead. Another method is to have a support vehicle follow riders, carrying all their supplies, food and water. This option allows bikers to cover large distances - 50 miles or more in a single day.

Out-and-Back Riding: This mode of biking involves riding a trail part of the way out and then back. A trail segment can be a completely new and different experience when ridden in the opposite direction. The best rule of thumb is to turn back when the water carried is half gone.

All segments of the Moab-Loma Route have good access points at the beginning and ending. Some segments can be accessed at a midpoint, but most cannot, making careful planning a necessity. If a rider has an emergency or equipment failure on the trail for which he or she is not prepared, there is often no mid-point at which to bail out. It is not the purpose to frighten potential desert travelers, only to make them realize the desert can be an unforgiving mistress for those who don't plan carefully.

It is impossible to overemphasize the importance of taking and drinking enough water when riding in the desert. This topic is discussed in detail in the chapter, "The Human Body Versus the Desert." Although riders cross the drainage lines of small creeks and streams on every segment of this trail, the presence of water varies depending on the season or the year's weather. Without knowing what conditions will exist on the trail, the best plan is to **carry all of the water needed.** Riders carrying water purification equipment can refill bottles when water is encountered, but should NOT plan on finding water on the trail.

A second note regarding desert water: simple halizone or other biological water treatment is not sufficient to make desert water potable. Often, desert water is contaminated with dissolved mineral salts such as selenium and arsenic, to name two. In order to make this water safe to drink, it is necessary to filter the water through a system designed to remove these toxic substances. See the "Equipment" chapter for more information on filtering devices.

Maps are another tool that every rider should carry. In addition to identifying the topography and geography along the trail, maps provide valuable information for a party with a lost or injured member. Each segment description has a listing of several different maps that can be used with this trail guide.

Chuck Nichols

HAZARDS

Knowing what hazards exist and being prepared for them can greatly enhance the experience of mountain biking through canyon country. Each rider should always read the trail description beforehand, to evaluate whether that segment matches his or her ability.

Vertical exposure is a hazard riders will encounter as they travel parts of this trail system. Some stretches consist of narrow, steep, rocky or partially washed-out road. Portions of the singletrack stretch of trail wind along cliffs or traverse steep hill sides. The combination of these conditions provides riding that is exciting but also dangerous. Exposure can turn a routine spill into a serious accident. Consequently, these areas have been rated Difficult.

Steep grades with rocky, sandy surfaces punctuate all segments of the Moab-Loma Route. They diminish traction and speed, which makes climbing and descending even more hazardous. These surfaces can also cause difficulty in estimating the time it takes to cover a given distance. Sand is especially bad in this respect. Plan on traveling - walking or riding - at a speed of about 1 mph when navigating deep sand. And don't underestimate the amount of energy needed to struggle through sand. Eat and drink in generous quantities when navigating any difficult terrain.

Flash floods are another potential hazard of which desert travelers should be aware. Several parts of this trail cross drywashes and travel through narrow canyons. Keep an eye on the sky, and if severe weather is approaching, be alert while traveling in or crossing drainages. Large storms can trigger flash floods that will travel for several miles. Always read the trail description ahead and use a map to avoid being caught unexpectedly.

Animals, wild and domestic, are a feature of canyon country that highlight each segment of this route. For the most part, wild animals are more afraid of humans than vice versa, and are seldom a threat. The rattlesnakes of this region are shy and retiring. In summer, they are also nocturnal and pose minimal threat to bikers. Cattle, on the other hand, can cause trouble. When riding on private land or open range, be aware of these animals and don't harass them. As a rule, they are docile and will move out of the way without being urged. In fact, just the approach of a bike on the trail usually causes them to panic and run. If they do not move, do a cowboy imitation, "Heyah!" If they still have not moved, rather than trying to face down an animal that outweighs you by several hundred pounds, go around. Be especially cautions of bulls. They can be aggressive and cantankerous.

Bugs are definitely a desert hazard. Other than their role in the ecosystem, there is not much good to say about the flies, mosquitoes and no-see-ums that infest the desert at certain times of the year. Be sure to carry plenty of bug repellent. Although scorpions also live in the desert, the species that inhabit this area are not the highly poisonous variety that live in Arizona. They can, however, deliver a painful sting. Black widow spiders are also desert dwellers, but pose little danger to mountain bikers.

Heat and cold in the desert can have severe effects on the human body. Always bring clothing for BOTH extremes. Although daytime desert temperatures can reach 100 + degrees, cold nights, especially in the spring and fall, can be miserable for someone unprepared. Always take a jacket and sweat pants, even in the summer. No one plans to spend a night out, but in case of emergency or weather change, it is better to be prepared. Heat is possibly the greatest desert hazard. It dehydrates bikers at an amazing rate, contributing to overheating. Keep the sun off the body with light-weight, light-colored clothing and a helmet or hat. In addition, drink plenty of water in order to keep sweating, and take lots of breaks in the shade. See the chapter on "The Human Body Versus the Desert" for more detailed information.

Private land is not a hazard on the trail, but because several parts of the Moab-Loma Route pass through private land, be respectful. The actions of a few careless individuals could jeopardize permissions given to ride across these private areas. Always stay on the trail. Be aware of livestock and treat them with respect. When passing through gates, leave them as you found them, and always be courteous to anyone else on the trail, letting vehicles pass when they approach. Aside from private land, the trail passes through BLM and National Forest land. Be aware of the camping guidelines for these areas, and remember that many of the rules that apply to private land apply here also. Do not ride off the trail, and obey all signs. A final word of caution: never travel alone in the desert. There are many unforeseen circumstances that can lead to disaster. Much of this trail is remote, and help is hours away.

THE HUMAN BODY VERSUS THE DESERT

WATER, WATER AND MORE WATER

The single most important thing riders must take into the desert is water. Even food is secondary to this precious, life-giving fluid. Riders traveling through this arid climate in high temperatures while exercising vigorously need copious quantities of water. It not only keeps the body alive, proper hydration increases physical performance and maintains mental functioning. DO NOT underestimate the amount of water the body requires while exercising in the desert.

The volume of water in the human body must be maintained within narrow limits. There are four factors at work to reduce water levels in the body when riding in the desert.

Digestion uses an approximate ratio of water to food of 1:1. Therefore, as riders eat to maintain energy levels, water is used to digest the food and carry the nutrients into the body.

Temperature regulation uses up body fluids at an alarming rate! As sweat runs down a rider's back and face, water needs to be replaced in order for the body to continue sweating. In a hot climate, sweating can reduce body weight by as much as 5% per hour.

Respiration is another key factor in dehydration. Studies indicate that water loss in an environment with 10% humidity - a desert average - can be as much as 1% of body weight per hour. Dry air is taken into the lungs and exhaled with a water content 12 times greater than when it was inhaled.

Exercise In addition to the above factors, increased respiration from exercise will obviously cause a rider to exhale moisture at a greater rate. Vigorous exercise increases the basal metabolic rate by 20-25 times, which in turn raises the core temperature of the body at a rate of one degree Centigrade every five minutes. The body's cooling system kicks in to avoid this potentially drastic temperature increase, again using water at an accelerated rate to produce sweat.

Experts on exercise physiology tell us that by the time a body experiences thirst, that body is already 1 quart low on fluid. Drinking frequently and regularly is therefore the key to avoiding dehydration. Don't wait for thirst to trigger a reaction. Make drinking a conscious effort. The average sedentary adult should consume about 2.5 liters of water daily. Exercise in a hot, arid climate increases that daily recommended intake approximately 6 times!

Again, it must be emphasized that it is impossible to take too much water when riding in the desert. A fluid loss of 4%-5% of the body's weight is sufficient to reduce blood plasma levels, affecting circulation, ability to sweat and cardiovascular function. Start a ride hydrated, drink plenty of fluids all day, and continue to replenish fluid levels in the evening. Doing those three things can help all riders maximize their performance and their fun.

FOOD AND EATING:

Eating enough food to maintain energy levels is another important consideration on long, strenuous rides. Often, the combination of enthusiasm and heat, followed by increasing exhaustion, can rob riders of their appetite. Eating is important, however, and shouldn't be left for the end of the day. This is especially true for riders planning multi-day adventures. Studies have indicated that once the glycogen levels (energy stores) in the muscles necessary for good performance are depleted, their replacement can take several days. Plan to avoid depletion.

During exercise, eat and drink monosaccharides and polysaccharides. In simple terms, saccharides are sugars. Monosaccharides are the easiest to digest, making them an especially good choice for exercise in desert heat. Monosaccharides include juices, sugars and honey. Polysaccharides take a bit longer to digest, but make good trail snacks as well. This group includes starches like rice, pasta, bread and cereals.

Before the ride, eat well-balanced meals, consuming polysaccharides the morning of the ride. Carbo-loading, contrary to popular myth, is a complex process, taking a week or longer to complete. Gorging on spaghetti the night before a ride is simply over-eating, and stresses the digestive system.

After the ride, again eat a well-balanced meal, with a small emphasis on fat. Fat is slow to digest (3-4 hours), making it ideal to eat the night before. Fatty acids and glycerol are converted into body energy once the polysaccharides are used up. Thus, fat intake is burned up during sustained exercise, rather than being stored as extra weight. Fats are found in cheese, butter, nuts, avocados and meats, for instance. Fat can benefit athletes when not consumed in excess. It rebuilds the body's stores of slow-release energy.

The wisest plan is to snack all day. Don't wait for hunger to set in. This method of eating on the trail prevents the body from depleting its energy stores, allowing riders to sustain an even energy level throughout the ride. And eating heartily in the evening, without over-eating, rebuilds energy levels for multi-day rides.

OTHER TIPS:

In addition to taking care of the body's physiological needs, other factors can help beat the desert heat. Obviously, light-colored, loose clothing can help in the fight to stay cool. A loose, white, long-sleeved shirt can be cooler than a sleeveless crop-top. Keeping the desert sun off the body is important. This method of dress will also prevent sunburn.

Timing the ride is also important. Spring and fall are the ideal seasons to enjoy the desert, but even then, daytime temperatures can exceed 90 degrees. To make the ride as easy as possible, leave early in the cool of the morning. Rest during the heat of the day and finish the ride later in the afternoon. There are many juniper and pinion trees along most stretches of the trail. Even a big rock will provide relief. Stop frequently to eat and drink in the shade to preserve physical well being.

SIGNS OF STRESS AND SERIOUS ILLNESS:

Paying attention to how the body feels is very important. The many signs of physical stress are not difficult to recognize and should not be ignored. The importance of drinking before thirsting, eating before hunger has beckoned, and avoiding sunburn have already been discussed . Other physical problems that require immediate attention include hypothermia and heat-illness.

Hypothermia can strike even in the summer. A rider caught unprepared in the rain could easily develop hypothermia. Cool night temperatures could also cause this alarming drop in the body's core temperature. Symptoms include poor coordination, slurred speech, mental dullness and confusion, and poor color in the face and extremities. Immediate action is required to reverse this life-threatening situation. Remedies include giving the victim hot fluids, adding heat through the use of a fire, or placing the victim in a sleeping bag with another person. Always remove wet clothing and/or add dry, warm clothing to prevent further heat-loss.

At the opposite end of the scale are the symptoms of heat-stress -- thirst, tiredness, grogginess, visual difficulties and cramps. If these symptoms are ignored, a serious and disabling series of complications called HEAT-ILLNESS can result. The three main types of heat-illness, in order of severity, are: HEAT-CRAMPS; HEAT-EXHAUSTION; AND HEAT-STROKE.

Heat-cramps are muscle spasms that occur during periods of exposure to heat and dehydration. They are caused by loss of salts during sweating. An elevated body temperature is not necessary to experience cramping. However, if the cramps are ignored a more serious situation will result. Relief for heat cramps includes drinking plenty of water and replenishing salt and electrolytes. Increasing salt and electrolyte intake prior to a ride can also help prevent this condition.

Heat-exhaustion is caused by poor circulation, combined with a reduction in blood volume due to extensive fluid loss. This condition is characterized by reduced sweat output, a weak and rapid pulse, dizziness and an overall feeling of weakness. Anyone experiencing these symptoms should immediately stop exercising, move to a shaded area and drink copious fluids.

Heat-stroke is the most complex and dangerous form of heat-illness. IT REQUIRES IMMEDIATE MEDICAL ATTENTION. Because riders on the trail do not have access to medical treatment, pay attention to the body, and don't get into this life-threatening situation. Heat-stroke is basically a failure of the heat regulating mechanisms of the body, caused by excessively high body temperatures. Symptoms include: cessation of sweating; dry, hot skin; and a dangerously high internal body temperature. This causes excessive strain on the circulatory system and, if left untreated, can result in permanent disability, central nervous system damage, or death from circulatory collapse. Heat-stroke is a serious medical emergency. While waiting for medical help, take immediate steps to lower the victim's temperature, including rubbing water over the skin, applying ice packs or immersing the victim in cold water.

The purpose of this chapter has not been to frighten riders, but to make them aware of their health. An amazing number of people encountered in the backcountry of canyon country are ill-prepared for the high-desert environment. Although it is difficult to admit, this author has been one of those people on occasion. The information presented here, if applied, will better prepare bikers for this and other backcountry bike routes, and enhance their desert experience. So much the better if a rider can make it up that last hill at the end of the day, or feel good on the second day of a strenuous ride. Although this sport has a serious side, the name of the game is still - MAXIMUM FUN!

Peggy and Bob Utesch at a Segment 2 viewpoint

EQUIPMENT

There is a large variety of equipment available for mountain biking. Some items are vital for survival, some make life on the trail easier, and some are just fun. The author likes to travel as light as possible, but also hates to be caught unprepared. This chapter contains a listing and discussion of equipment. Use this information as a guideline to enhance individual preferences.

Bike computers: These high tech devices come highly recommended. I have yet to find a map containing all the roads encountered. Because distance is difficult to judge in the desert, a computer is invaluable for helping locate current position. Many brands are available. Select one with the features that best meet individual preferences and needs.

Map and compass: Never venture into the backcountry without a map and compass and the knowledge of how to use these tools. As mentioned under the computer heading, many maps are not current. Should a rider become lost or confused at an unmarked intersection, a map, especially when used with a bike computer's odometer, can abate that cloud of confusion. It is also nice to know the names of the geographic features encountered.

Clothing: A helmet is essential equipment for backcountry adventures. Some might balk, thinking head gear is too hot for the desert. Think of it this way -- one unfortunate roll of a rock and the resulting head injury could be life-threatening. Wearing a light colored hat or visor under a helmet can also keep sun off the face.

Riding gloves, especially the type with gel padding in the palms, are nice for rough desert roads. They also protect the hands in the event of a fall.

Biking shorts or tights for cooler weather are highly recommended. Regular shorts are fine for short rides. However, for long days on the trail, shorts or tights with a padded crotch specifically designed for biking can greatly reduce fatigue due to discomfort.

Sunglasses: Protection from the sun, glare, hazards on the trail and bugs are four good reasons never to ride without eye protection.

Bug repellent and sunscreen: Anyone foolish enough to venture into the desert without BOTH of these items is ... well ... suffice it to say, he or she won't make that mistake twice!

First aid: There are several levels of first aid. For a trained Emergency Medical Technician, an advanced first aid kit is useful. Yet for someone without medical training, the contents of an advanced kit will be useless. As a minimum, carry the items listed below, or found in first aid kits available at bike or mountaineering shops. Taking a first aid class is also a good idea.

* band aids
* 4x4 gauze pads
* antiseptic
* chemical ice pack
* butterflies
* pain relievers
* compress

* Bactine
* tweezers
* antacids
* cloth tape
* needle
* sunscreen
* anti-bacterial ointment

Tools: First aid for bicycles is more complicated. The ideal tool kit is a compromise between weight and necessity. The list below on the left is a bare minimum. The list on the right notes optional items. What a rider takes depends on the length of the ride and the terrain. Choose the kit contents carefully.

Allen wrenches to fit each bike
Wrenches to fit nuts/bolts on each bike
Spare tube
Tire irons
Spoke wrench
Patch kit
Duct tape
Lubricant (Tri-Flo or WS-40)
Screwdriver to fit the derailleur
Spare tire *
Chain breaker
Extra chain
Spokes
Crank arm wrenches

* Not all brands of tires fold for packing.
  Tire liners are recommended for desert riding.

THE FIFTEEN DESERT ESSENTIALS - A CHECK-LIST:

1. Water, Water, Water
2. Food
3. Map and compass
4. First aid kit
5. Space blanket or tarp
6. Fire starter (waterproof matches or lighter)
7. Sunscreen
8. Bug repellent
9. Extra clothing (hat, jacket, sweatclothes or tights)
10. Bike tools
11. 50 Feet of 4mm cord
12. Knife
13. Flashlight or headlamp
14. Mirror or metal reflector
15. Water filtering device

Chuck Nichols

BACKCOUNTRY ETHICS

Ethics is a topic that evokes very strong feeling on the part of this author. The future of backcountry use depends on visitors caring enough to protect our precious recreational lands. Today, many wilderness areas and national parks have closed, or are on the verge of closing, their boundaries to mountain bikers. This unfortunate circumstance has been brought about by a few inconsiderate individuals who have caused damage and erosion to unspoiled terrain by riding off trails, and who have been disrespectful of other backcountry users.

The desert is a fragile ecosystem, much like the arctic tundra. The actions of a few thoughtless individuals can have a negative impact on the land that lasts for many years. Please take the time to learn about the desert so as to appreciate its subtle beauty and protect its natural wonders. Following is a discussion of basic ethical considerations. Abide by these guidelines, and encourage others to do so as well. That way, the desert can maintain its timeless mystique, and we can all enjoy its wonders for years to come.

Yielding right-of-way: Uphill traffic always has the right-of-way in the backcountry. When other vehicles or bikers are encountered, uphill traffic should be allowed to proceed first. Another good idea is to let motorized vehicles pass at any time. In most cases, they are traveling faster and will be out of the way quickly.

Staying on roads and trails: Much of the desert consists of barren sand and soil. Without the ground cover of the prairies and mountains, deserts depend on *cryptogamic soil* to prevent erosion. Desert soil is permeated with living organisms that hold the soil in place through rain and wind. An inch of *cryptogamic soil* takes decades to form. It can be destroyed in an instant by a bicycle wheel or footprint. This destruction then leads to erosion. Damage is visible in Canyonlands, Arches and Capitol Reef national parks where bikers have ridden off the roads in order to avoid steep, sandy or otherwise difficult stretches. In their "macho" -- the fact that they didn't have to walk -- they have severely damaged the fragile ecosystem of the desert. These scars take years to heal. ALWAYS STAY ON ROADS AND TRAILS, and leave the timeless beauty of the desert undisturbed.

Camping. The Bureau of Land Management has established primitive campsites along the Kokopelli's Trail. These sites include fire grates, picnic tables and pit toilets. Campers are urged to use these designated sites rather than make new ones. If it is not possible to use a BLM site, the ethical rule in the desert is to camp in a previously used site, thus minimizing further impact on the desert. When not camping in a BLM site with a fire grate, use of a camp stove or fire pan (metal pan or trash can lid) for cooking is preferable to building a fire on the ground. Campers are also encouraged to bring their own firewood or briquettes. Pack out the ashes, and the campsites will be clean and enjoyable for future users. Fires built on the ground or in old fire rings, and using wood from the desert, are NOT ethical! Fire rings scar the landscape and wood is scarce. However, fire rings are found throughout this area. Remember, just because someone else was ignorant does not justify additional inconsideration.

Disposal of human waste: In the arid climate of the desert, human waste takes a long time to decompose. Bury excrement at least 6 inches deep and 100 feet away from water drainages, campsites and rivers. Another caution -- the old rule of burning toilet paper is no longer accepted. This practice has been responsible for devastating fires caused by careless burning. The goal is to answer the call of nature, but leave no trace for future trail users. Whenever possible, use the BLM primitive toilets along the trail to avoid contamination of the desert landscape.

The key to responsible travel in the desert is low impact. Bring EVERYTHING needed for the trip and PACK IT ALL OUT when the trip is over. Leaving NOTHING behind protects the desert's beauty.

HOW TO USE THIS GUIDEBOOK

At the beginning of each trail segment is a listing of specific trail information. This listing provides, at a glance, the specifications of each of the six trail segments. This format enables riders to easily compare their skills and objectives with the challenges of the ride. In addition, an elevation chart is given to help riders visualize the trail.

The map accompanying each segment provides general information about the trail. The route is marked on the map using a dashed line to indicate singletrack and a solid line to indicate dirt road. Available supplementary maps are listed under **Maps**. Most of these can be obtained in Moab from various retail outlets, local visitor centers or BLM offices. Some can be found at similar outlets in Grand Junction.

The next heading is **Trail Summary**. There, a general description of the trail is given, discussing both the highlights and difficulties to be encountered.

Following the Trail Summary are two **Mileage Logs**. The first log describes the trail traveling west to east, Moab-to-Loma. The second describes traveling east to west, Loma-to-Moab. The described route is exciting and challenging ridden in either direction. Most major intersections on the trail are marked with a BLM trail marker. However, some are not. In addition, some markers may have been vandalized. The prevalence of mineral exploration roads not shown on most maps can also be confusing. The mileage logs are listings of landmarks, intersection directions and points of interest designed to keep the rider on track and make the most of the trip. Supplementary maps can be useful. Also, keep in mind that mileages will vary depending on the odometer, its calibration, tire inflation and other variables. Use the mileages only as close approximations.

SEGMENT 1
Moab to Castle Valley

Distance: Main Route - 21.1 miles; Alternate Route - 25.4 miles

Difficulty: Easy - 6.2 mi; Moderate - 11.7 mi; Difficult - 3.2mi

Time: 4 - 7 Hours

Elevations: West - 4600 ft; High - 8300 ft; East - 6500 ft

Maps: **USGS** 7 1/2': Rill Creek UT; Warner Lake UT
      BLM: Moab NW/4 1:100,000 metric
      Wasatch Publishers: *Canyon Country* ORV Trail Map #7
      Trails Illustrated: Moab Area Mountain Bike Routes

TRAIL SUMMARY:

This segment of the Moab-Loma Route ascends out of Moab on a paved and graded-gravel road called the Sand Flats Road. As a dirt road, then rough off-road vehicle trail, it climbs through a spectacular desert panorama into the foothills of the La Sal Mountains. Fantastic views of the canyon country surrounding Moab -- including the Arches area to the north and Canyonlands Park to the southwest -- are just some of the highlights. In addition, riders will pass scenic Negro Bill and Rill Canyons and an enchanting series of sandstone spires. An arch is also visible near the summit of an eroded slickrock dome. Additional arches are in the vicinity for those wishing to hike. The east end of the trail travels along the paved Castle Valley Road. The Priest and Nuns and Castle Tower rock formations rise majestically over Castle Valley in the distance. Before reaching Castle Valley, the route travels a 3.2 mile stretch of difficult ORV trail that often resembles singletrack. This stretch delivers riders to Porcupine Rim where a splendid view of Castle Valley unfolds. Riders wishing to avoid this difficult stretch can bypass it by staying on the Sand Flats Road. The alternate route increases the distance of the ride by 4.3 miles as it travels through the most scenic and historic stretch of the Sand Flats Road. Watch for an old pioneer homestead on this route.

To access the trail from its western end, travel east off of Main Street in Moab on 100 North Street for four blocks to the intersection of 100 North Street and 400 East Street. Turn right onto 400 East and go approximately 1/2 mile to the intersection of 400 East and Mill Creek Road. Turn left on Mill Creek Road and climb a grade. In approximately 1/2 mile, angle left at a "Y" intersection and climb past the cemetery on what is now the Sand Flats Road. Continue ascending on paved road past the dump. **Outside Magazine** readers voted this the most scenic dump in America! Continue to the parking lot at the entrance to the Slickrock Bike Trail. Park and begin riding east on the Sand Flats Road.

To access this trail segment at its eastern end, turn off of Utah 128 onto the Castleton-Gateway Road, approximately 15.5 miles east of Moab. Follow this road about 10.6 miles to where it intersects the La Sal Loop Road. Begin riding here, on the La Sal Loop Road.

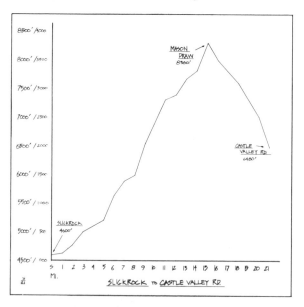

MILEAGE LOG: WEST TO EAST

0.0   Begin riding east on the Sand Flats Road. Immediately climb through the petrified sand dune formations and small canyons that form this area. BLM trail markers appear every mile or so, verifying the route.

6.4   Negro Bill Canyon is visible to the left of the road. Pass a stock-watering tank and travel through a low pass which takes the rider away from Negro Bill Canyon on the left and immediately toward Rill Canyon which appears on the right. Note the view back toward Moab.

22

MAP OF SEGMENT 1

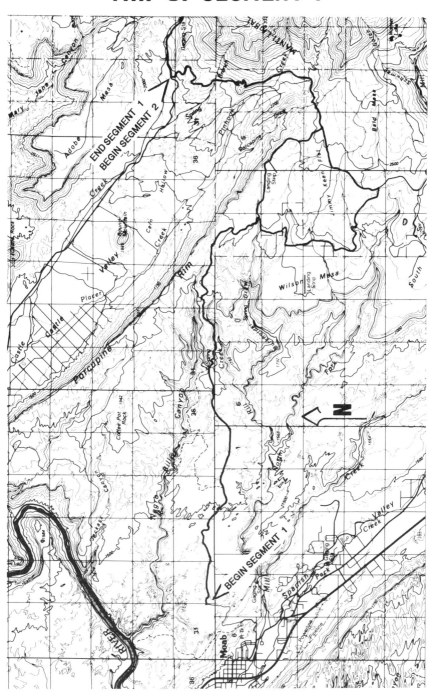

8.9 A spectacular formation of sandstone spires comes into view ahead on the climb out of Rill Canyon. An arch will also soon become visible in the end of an eroded slickrock dome.

9.4 Cross an expanse of slickrock approximately 0.1 mile long, and begin the final steep climb out of Rill Canyon.

10.1 Enter Maloy Park, where a fantastic view of the Arches area is to the northwest, with the Canyon Rims area and Henry Mountains to the southwest.

10.3 Cross a cattleguard and the National Forest boundary. There is a log corral on the right side of the trail. The plant community has changed from the sage/pinion/juniper landscape of the lower desert to old-growth Ponderosa pine and pinion pine forest.

11.0 The La Sal Mountains are now visible ahead. As the road forks, stay to the right. The fork to the left is a short spur that ends at Porcupine Rim with a great view.

11.6 The trail is descending slightly, approaching a flat, hairpin turn. From here, aspen trees are visible beside the road ahead, their white trunks and quaking leaves confirming the altitude gain. Begin watching for the BLM trail marker on the left of the road, where this bike route leaves the Sand Flats Road.

F. A. Barnes

Main Route:

11.7   The main Moab-Loma Route turns off of the Sand Flats Road to the left, just beyond the hairpin curve. A BLM trail marker designates this junction. The route climbs a steep embankment then continues ascending in the form of a deeply rutted ORV trail as it travels toward Porcupine Rim. Along this route are spectacular views of Castle Valley and Porcupine Draw. This 3.2-mile stretch is rated Difficult, and those wishing to avoid it should use the Alternate Route description.

13.3   The trail approaches Porcupine Draw overlook as it winds along the canyon rim.

13.7   An abandoned mine, complete with rusted truck chassis and old, rickety shack, is visible. This stretch of the trail is mostly hard-packed clay and would be a nightmare when wet. The trail passes through an oak-brush corridor on the east end of this segment, as the trail joins the La Sal Loop Road in the foothills of the La Sal Mountains.

14.9 (19.2*) The ORV trail enters the La Sal Loop Road where the view is breathtaking in all directions. The wooded slopes of the La Sal Mountains are lush and particularly beautiful in the fall when the oak-brush and aspen trees have turned color. To the northwest, the distinctive Castle Tower-Priest & Nuns formation is visible. Turn left on the paved road and begin an exciting descent. Some of the pavement is broken, so take care on the switchbacks where speeds of 30 + mph are possible. There are several shady stretches of road, as it passes Harpole Mesa. Watch for ice in these areas in the early spring and late fall. Tight turns, cattleguards and traffic can be dangerous at high speeds as well.

21.1   The La Sal Loop Road intersects the Castleton-Gateway Road, marking the end of this segment.

Alternate Route:

11.7   Continue riding on the Sand Flats Road.

12.4   A private access road takes off to the right. Stay left as an historic homestead becomes visible on a hill to the left.

13.0   At a fork in the road, turn left.

13.5   An open meadow affords a beautiful view to the right.

14.2   Begin gently climbing into the foothills of the La Sals.

15.6   Cattleguard crossing.

16.9   Intersect with the paved La Sal Loop Road. Turn left.

19.0   The main Moab-Loma bike trail comes into the La Sal Loop Road from the left. To continue, see Main Route description at mile 14.9. Alternate Route mileages appear with an asterisk (*).

MILEAGE LOG: EAST TO WEST

0.0   Begin riding this segment of the Moab-Loma Route at the intersection of the Castleton-Gateway Road and the La Sal Loop Road. Climb through upper Castle Valley to the foothills of the La Sal Mountains on the paved road. This prolonged climb is technically easy but physically strenuous.

3.5   Ascending through Harpole Mesa, cross a cattleguard. Several stretches in this area are shaded, so watch for ice in the early spring and late fall. Continue climbing on switchbacks as fantastic views open up in every direction.

5.5   The climb becomes less steep, and the distinctive Castle Tower-Priest & Nuns formation is visible on the right. To the left, the aspen and pine slopes of the La Sal Mountains grace the scene.

End of short spur to Porcupine Rim
F. A. Barnes

26

Main Route:

6.2   The main Moab-Loma Route leaves the La Sal Loop Road to the
        right on a rough and rutted ORV trail that immediately de-
        scends through an oak-brush corridor. Look for the BLM trail
        maker at the turn-off. Wind along the rim of Porcupine Draw,
        enjoying a spectacular view. This 3.2-mile stretch of road is
        rated Difficult. However, the scenery is well worth the effort.
        The trail surface is mostly packed clay. The east end of the trail
        is deeply rutted, making it necessary for riders to alternate
        tracks. For those wishing to avoid this stretch, see Alternate
        Route.

8.2   An abandoned mining area is visible, complete with rusted truck
        chassis and old, rickety mine shack.

8.7   The trail travels along the mesa rim, affording a breathtaking
        view of Porcupine Draw and Castle Valley. The last 1/2 mile or
        so is a steep, rutted decline, dropping back onto the Sand Flats
        Road.

9.4 (13.7*) At the intersection with the Sand Flats Road, follow the
        BLM trail marker to the right and go around a flat, hairpin turn
        as the road begins to climb.

10.1 (14.4*) As the road forks, continue to the right, passing under
        some power lines and proceeding into Maloy Park.

10.8 (15.1*) Cross a cattleguard at the National Forest boundary. Note
        the log corral on the left.

11.1 (15.4*) Descend into Rill Canyon. The trail surface is punctuated
        with short, sandy pockets as well as stretches of slickrock.
        Some of the rock displays ancient water-ripples. Continue to
        descend next to Rill Canyon, enjoying the broad view of the
        entire Moab Valley.

11.5 (15.8*) The trail is nearing some scenic sandstone spires. Notice
        the small arch on the skyline at the end of a eroding dome of
        slickrock, all visible to the left of the road. Arches National
        Park, the Canyon Rims area and the Henry Mountains can be
        seen ahead in the distance.

14.7 (19.0*) Climb to a short, narrow pass where the trail leaves the Rill Canyon drainage. Negro Bill Canyon becomes visible on the right as the trail passes stock-watering tanks.

15 - 21.1 (19.3 - 25.4*) The last part of this trail segment continues to descend on a good, gravel road through small canyons and the same kind of petrified sand dunes that form the famous Slickrock Bike Trail. This segment ends at the parking lot of the Slickrock Trail, although riders can continue on this road for approximately 3.7 miles into Moab.

Alternate Route:

6.2   Continue on the paved La Sal Loop Road, past the Moab-Loma Main Route turnoff, for an additional 2.3 miles.

8.5   Turn right onto the Sand Flats Road at an intersection marked by a Forest Service sign. The road is now improved dirt.

9.8   Cattleguard crossing and excellent views.

11.9   A large meadow opens up on the left with views of the Canyon Rims area and the Henry Mountains to the southwest.

12.4   At a fork in the road, stay right.

View of Negro Bill Canyon from Segment 1 - F. A. Barnes

13.0   Stay right again as the road to the left is private.

13.7   The main Moab-Loma Route enters the Sand Flats Road from the right, just past some aspen trees which are also to the right of the road. Continue around a flat, hairpin turn on the Sand Flats Road.

OPTIONAL RIDING

1.   Porcupine Rim Trail, described in "*Canyon Country* **MOUNTAIN BIKING**," by F.A. Barnes and Tom Kuehne.

2.   La Sal Loop Road. From the point where the Moab-Loma Route joins the Sand Flats Road, or at the intersection of the Sand Flats Road and the La Sal Loop Road on the Alternate Route, the La Sal Loop Road can be ridden back to Moab in either direction. Either route is mostly downhill and about 25 miles back to town on paved road.

View from short spur to Porcupine Rim - F. A. Barnes

SEGMENT 2
Castle Valley to Fisher Valley

Distance:	23.8 Miles
Difficulty:	Moderate - 20 miles; Difficult - 4 miles
Time:	5 - 8 Hours
Elevation:	West - 6400 ft; High - 8600 ft; East - 5600 ft

Maps: **USGS** 7 1/2': Fisher Valley UT; Blue Chief Mesa UT; Dewey UT
BLM: Moab NW/4 1:100,000 metric
Wasatch Publishers: *Canyo... Country* ORV Trail Map #7
Trails Illustrated: Moab Area Mountain Bike Routes

TRAIL SUMMARY:

The Moab-Loma Route, as it travels from Castle Valley to Fisher Valley, combines the beauty of the La Sal Mountain foothills with the magic of the desert. The trail takes riders across Fisher and North Beaver Mesas, makes a spectacular descent through the upper end of Thompson Canyon, around Cowhead Hill, and ends in Fisher Valley. There is also an abundance of fantastic, optional day-rides in the area, making it a great place to spend several days exploring. The scenery ranges from pine and aspen forests on the slopes of the La Sals, to a sage-juniper-cactus landscape on the lower desert floor. Old growth Ponderosa pines dot the landscape in several areas, harboring the secrets of the last 200 years. In addition, deer and several varieties of lizards can be seen darting across the trail. Especially beautiful are the collared lizards with their bright yellow heads and black-banded necks. Coyote and puma tracks are not uncommon, although seeing one of these largely-nocturnal animals is rare. The coyote talks at night, however, so be listening for his conversation while sitting around the campfire or dreaming through the desert night.

To access the east end of this trail segment, take the Castleton-Gateway Road off of Utah 128, approximately 15.5 miles east of Moab. Travel north on the Gateway Road about 10.5 miles to where it intersects the La Sal Loop Road. Begin riding east on the Castleton-Gateway Road.

To access the north end of this segment, take the Onion Creek Road south from Utah 128. This road is signed as the "Taylor Livestock/Fisher Valley Ranch Road." Drive approximately 13 miles up the spectacular Onion Creek drainage. This dirt road crosses shallow Onion Creek 26 times before climbing a narrow ridge into the upper end of Fisher Valley. Come to the 3-way intersection of Onion Creek Road, Cottonwood Canyon Trail (left) and Thompson Canyon Trail (right). Begin riding toward the Fisher Valley Ranch at an intersection, designated by a BLM trail marker.

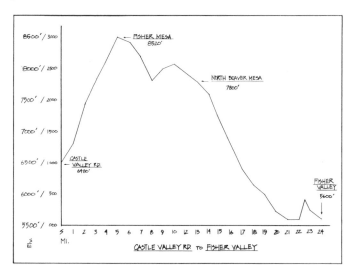

MILEAGE LOG: WEST TO EAST

0.0   To begin this scenic ride, proceed east on the Castleton -Gateway Road to where it intersects the La Sal Loop Road. The first several miles are a steady climb to the top of Fisher Mesa where the pavement ends.

1.6   Cross a cattleguard and pass the trailhead for Bachelor Basin as well as a creek.

2.5   The pavement ends and the road becomes a graded gravel road with lots of washboards. Watch for deer in this area.

MAP OF SEGMENT 2

END SEGMENT 2
BEGIN SEGMENT 3

END SEGMENT 1
BEGIN SEGMENT 2

3.6 The road begins to level out. The Henry Mountains, Canyon-lands and the Canyon Rims area are visible to the west. The oak-brush landscape becomes dotted with old growth Ponderosa pine as the trail nears the top of Fisher Mesa.

5.8 The climb up Fisher Mesa has topped out. Fisher Mesa and Fisher Valley are visible to the left with North Beaver Mesa visible on the right. Begin descending, still on gravel road.

7.7 At an intersection marked "Dons Lake - North Beaver Mesa - Gateway, Colorado," stay left toward North Beaver Mesa on the Polar Mesa Road. The road is a double track ORV trail with a packed sediment surface.

8.1 A bridge crosses an unnamed creek where cattle corrals are on the right. The surface is red, powdered sediment for a short distance, as the road begins to climb. Coyote, puma and deer tracks are prevalent in this area.

9-10 The trail crosses the upper end of North Beaver Mesa where shady rest spots are available under the Ponderosa pines.

10.9 Cross a cattleguard. A view opens up ahead with Thompson Canyon visible on the right. Hideout Canyon and Cottonwood Canyon can be seen on the left.

11.9 Arrive at the intersection of Polar Mesa Trail and Thompson Canyon Road. The Moab-Loma Route continues left along the Thompson Canyon Road.

13.6 Come to a sign at an intersection stating "Fisher Mesa 9 miles - Highway 128, 21 miles." Follow the BLM trail marker to the left, heading toward Highway 128.

15.2 An alternate scenic overlook loop turns off to the left that is definitely worth taking. The Fisher Towers formation also becomes visible.

15.9 The road forks. Follow the BLM trail marker and begin descending.

16-20 At mile 16, begin a steep descent around Cowhead Hill. The first 1.5 miles are challenging, combining water ruts with large rocks, steps, loose rock and sand.

18.6   The grade becomes less steep, although some technical stretches exist as the trail dips and climbs across small hills on its way to a creek bottom. Cottonwoods are visible ahead where the trail crosses a creek.

20.8   Cross a small, spring-fed tributary of Cottonwood Creek. Large cottonwoods provide shade for rest and refreshments.

21.0   Cross another small spring and begin climbing the low, roller coaster hills that mark the ascent out of Cottonwood Canyon.

21.1   At a fork in the road, stay right. There is no BLM marker at this intersection.

22.5   Begin a short, steep hill climb to a notch, visible ahead on the horizon.

22.6   Finish climbing out of the creek bottom on a steep stretch having one switchback. Pass through a fence and gate at the top of the notch, and enter private land. The beautiful panorama of upper Fisher Valley is visible from the hill top. Fisher Valley Ranch is on the left. Continue by riding down a moderately steep hill to a "Y" intersection.

23.4   Pass through another fence with a large, wooden gate. Leave the gate as you find it.

23.8   Riding along the Thompson Canyon Trail, intersect with the Onion Creek Road. This route segment ends at this point, designated by a trail marker. To reach Utah 128, head west on the Onion Creek Road.

View of Castle Valley from Segment 1 - F. A. Barnes

0.0   The Onion Creek Road intersects with the Moab-Loma Bicycle Trail in the upper end of Fisher Valley, approximately 13 miles from Utah 128. A BLM trail marker at this 3-way intersection designates the beginning of this segment, also known as the Thompson Canyon Trail. Begin riding to the right (east) toward the Fisher Valley Ranch.

0.4   Pass through a fence with a large gate, leaving the gate as it is found. Riders are now on private land.

1.0   At a "Y" intersection, turn left, away from the ranch, and begin climbing toward a notch on the horizon.

1.2   Pass through a fence and gate at the top of the hill and immediately begin a steep descent into a creek bottom. The trail is now back on public land.

2.7   At a fork in the road, stay left and go downhill. There is not a BLM marker at this intersection.

2.8   Cross a small spring and continue descending.

3.0   Cross a spring-fed tributary of Cottonwood Creek. This is an excellent, shaded place to rest, drink and eat. Begin climbing out of the drainage over hilly terrain with short, technical stretches.

5.2   The road becomes steeper as it climbs Cowhead Hill to North Beaver Mesa. The next several miles are rated Difficult, as the trail grade steepens over a surface of loose rock, sand, steps and water ruts. The view is spectacular!

7.9   The climb tops out and the Fisher Towers formation is visible to the north. Thompson Canyon is on the left, with Hideout Canyon on the right as the route enters the old growth Ponderosa pine forest on the top of North Beaver Mesa. Ample shade is available here to rest and recuperate after a difficult climb.

11.9   This intersection of the Thompson Canyon and Polar Mesa Roads marks the 1/2 way point of this ride. Stay right, as designated by the BLM trail marker.

12.9   Cross a cattleguard as the trail becomes packed sediment. Coyote, deer and puma tracks are visible in the powdery road surface.

15.7   Cross a bridge where cattle pens are directly to the left of the road.

16.1   Encounter an intersection and sign marked "Dons Lake - North Beaver Mesa - Gateway Colorado." Turn right, toward Fisher Mesa on a graded gravel road.

17.5   Begin climbing, more steeply, toward Fisher Mesa on a washboarded road.

18.7   The top of Fisher Mesa is the highest point on the Moab-Loma Route. An exhilarating view of Fisher Valley and the Castle Tower-Priest and Nuns formation is to the north. The La Sal Mountains dominate the landscape to the south. Rest here in the shade of the pines before beginning a rapid descent.

21.3   Although a short stretch of pavement precedes this point, continuous pavement begins here. Riders can reach speeds of 30 + mph in this area. Watch for deer and cattleguards.

22.2   CATTLEGUARD!

23.8   Riders are traveling on the Castleton-Gateway Road. This segment of the route ends where this road intersects the La Sal Loop Road.

Thompson Canyon and Polar Mesa, Segment 2 - F. A. Barnes

OPTIONAL RIDING:

1. Taylor Livestock/Fisher Valley Ranch Rd. (Onion Creek).

2. Beaver Basin ORV trail

3. Fisher Mesa ORV trail

4. Adobe Mesa ORV trail

The first three rides are described in "*Canyon Country* **Mountain Biking**" by F.A. Barnes and Tom Kuehne.

The Adobe Mesa trail is described in the book, "*Canyon Country* **Off-Road Vehicle Trails - Arches and La Sals Areas,**" by F.A. Barnes.

Segment 2 near Polar Mesa - F. A. Barnes

View from beyond end of Adobe Mesa spur trail

F. A. Barnes

SEGMENT 3
Fisher Valley to Dewey Bridge

Distance: 18 Miles

Difficulty: Moderate - 16.5; Difficult - 6.5

Time: 6-9 Hours

Elevation: West - 5600 ft; High - 6400 ft; East - 4100 ft

Maps: **USGS** 7 1/2': Fisher Valley UT; Blue Chief Mesa UT; Dewey UT
BLM: Moab NW/4 1:100,000 metric
Wasatch Publishers: *Canyon Country* ORV Trail Map #7
Trails Illustrated: Moab Area Mountain Bike Routes

TRAIL SUMMARY:

This segment of the Moab-Loma Route is the most remote. Between Fisher Valley and Dewey Bridge, the terrain is spectacular. The trail surface, where coyote, cat and deer tracks are visible, alternates between packed sediments, steep grades of loose rock with sandstone steps, and graded gravel road. The route crosses two small, steep canyons, both named Cottonwood Canyon. These canyons are beautiful and technically difficult, providing an exciting challenge for more experienced riders. For less experienced riders, the magical scenery is well worth the time it takes to walk the difficult stretches in these small canyons. One of the canyons can be circumnavigated, indicated as Alternate Route in the text. For those using the Trails Illustrated Map, this Alternate Route is the trail marked on that map, although it is not the official designated route. Several varieties of lizards can be seen in this area, including the large and brightly-colored collared lizard. Watch for them as they often sunbathe beside the trail. Beginning in the high desert on the west end, and ending near the confluence of the Dolores and Colorado Rivers, a variety of beautiful rock formations highlight the ride. In addition, a small area of slickrock is accessible above Dewey Bridge for those who wish to play. Remember not to ride through cryptogamic soil or potholes as these are fragile ecosystems. There is also an abundance of spur trails to explore, making it possible to spend several days in this area.

The east access is off of Utah 128 where the highway crosses the Colorado River at historic Dewey Bridge. Parking is available on the Moab side of the new bridge, near the base of the old Dewey suspension bridge. Much of the land on both sides of the highway is private, so be courteous.

To access the trail traveling in the Moab-Loma direction, turn off of Utah 128 and travel north on the Taylor Livestock/Fisher Valley Ranch Road for about 13 miles. This is also known as the Onion Creek Road. This good, dirt road crosses shallow Onion Creek 26 times before climbing out of a spectacular canyon into upper Fisher Valley. At the upper end of the valley, the Fisher Valley Ranch Road intersects with another road. This intersection is marked by a BLM trail marker. Begin riding east at this intersection, away from the Fisher Valley Ranch, visible to the south.

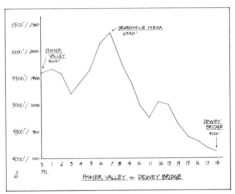

Upper Fisher Valley - F. A. Barnes

0.0   Begin riding left at the intersection of the Fisher Valley Ranch Road and the Cottonwood Canyon ORV trail. Ride away from the Fisher Valley Ranch, as designated by the BLM trail marker. The trail surface is packed sediment.

0.4   A large rock below a butte marks a "Y" intersection. Travel left, as indicated by the BLM trail marker. Proceed around the butte on the left.

1.1   Past the butte, a view of Hideout Canyon becomes visible.

1.6   Begin descending into the first of two Cottonwood Canyons. The trail surface is now loose rock and sandstone.

2.1   At an intersection where the BLM trail marker can be confusing, stay left, and continue descending into Cottonwood Canyon. The right fork heads back around the bluff and drops into Hideout Canyon.

3.0   Reach the bottom of this descent where the beautiful eroded walls of Cottonwood Canyon are on the right. Immediately begin an ascent that most riders will have to walk. The trail is very steep, even for a motorized vehicle, with large loose rocks that also make hiking difficult. Luckily this hill is only 0.2 mile long.

3.2   Top out of this radical climb and continue ascending on better trail. Wonderful views ahead and to the right fuel the soul.

4.1   Dip and climb away from the rim of Cottonwood Canyon to where a "T" intersection divides the trail. Go left, turning away from the first of the two Cottonwood Canyons.

6.0   Near the end of this climb a pullout is on the right. Stop to eat and drink here while enjoying a spectacular view that includes the Entrada slickrock of the Dolores River Canyon. The road improves from here, and the grade becomes less steep.

6.6   At another "T" intersection, continue straight through.

6.7   Pass an old drill pad to the right of the trail while ascending Sevenmile Mesa. Drink in the rewarding views of canyon country!

MAP OF SEGMENT 3

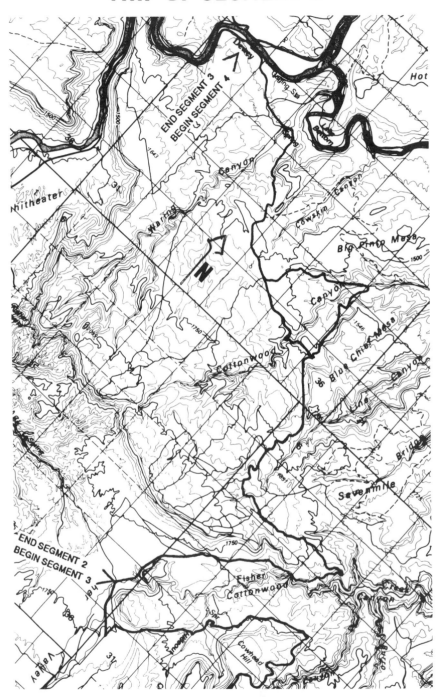

Lower Cottonwood Canyon, Segment 3 - Peggy Utesch

7.1   Beautiful Line Canyon is on the right, directly below the road, as the route descends Sevenmile Mesa toward Blue Chief Mesa. Several mineral exploration trails intersect the road in this area. Stay on what is obviously the main gravel road.

9.3   Continue descending toward the scenic Entrada formations at the tip of Blue Chief Mesa. The second Cottonwood Canyon becomes visible on the left.

Main Route:

10.4   The designated Moab-Loma Route leaves the gravel road to the left. This intersection is not particularly obvious, so watch for the BLM trail marker. The descent into the second Cottonwood Canyon is steep and could be dangerous for less experienced riders. The road is narrow and the exposure is great. This old, overgrown ORV trail, cluttered with large rocks, drops rapidly. The scenery is definitely worth the effort, even if it must be walked. Riders wishing to avoid this little jewel should take the Alternate Route described later.

10.7   A notch is visible on the horizon. The trail will eventually pass through this notch.

11.3   Go through a fence before crossing a spring fed creek at the bottom of the canyon. Immediately begin climbing. The ascent is not as steep or dangerous, because the trail has a better surface and fewer obstacles.

43

12.4   Once out of the canyon, pass through a heavy fence and continue gently ascending to the top of the grade. Shade is available through here, so stop to drink and snack.

12.6 (14.8*) At a "Y" intersection, take either fork to intersect with the main gravel road. Turn left onto the road where a needle-and-fin rock formation becomes visible ahead. The trail travels through roller-coaster hills all the way to the Colorado River. Use caution on this descent since loose gravel and washboarded road can be dangerous at high speeds.

14.0 (18.2*) A road turns off to the right. Stay on the main road and enjoy the views of Little Pinto Mesa on the right and Waring Canyon on the left.

15.7 (19.9*) Access to an area of slickrock riding is to the right. Don't ride through potholes or cryptogamic soil.

18.0 (22.2*) Upon reaching the parking area at the base of the historic Dewey Bridge, this segment is finished. Be sure to read the historical marker at the bridge and be respectful of the private land surrounding this area.

Alternate Route:

10.4   Stay on the main gravel road, NOT turning at the BLM trail marker into the second Cottonwood Canyon.

12.4   At an intersection, turn left. The right fork continues toward Utah Bottoms and the historic Dolores River Ford, both of which are on private land.

14.6   Continue toward the right at a "Y" intersection where the Main Route enters the gravel road from the left. Rejoin the Main Route description, where Alternate Route mileages are indicated with an asterisk (*).

MILEAGE LOG: EAST TO WEST

0.0   Begin riding this segment of the Moab-Loma Route on the Moab side of the Colorado River at the base of historic Dewey Bridge, directly off Utah 128. Ride south on a graded gravel road that climbs over roller-coaster hills.

Slickrock playground, Segment 3 - F. A. Barnes

2.3   Access slickrock riding on the left side of the road at this point. Don't ride on the cryptogamic soil or through potholes.

4.0   A side road comes in from the right. Stay on the main gravel road.

5.4   Two roads turn off to the right within 100 feet of each other. Take either turn and begin gently descending into the first of two Cottonwood Canyons. The road surface becomes packed sediment. Although the canyon is rated Difficult, less experienced riders should walk through it, as the scenery is fantastic. Riders wishing to avoid this Cottonwood Canyon should take the Alternate Route.

5.6   Pass through a large fence with Cottonwood Canyon visible ahead.

6.3   Travel through a notch and begin a steep descent over sand and loose rock, leading to the bottom of this canyon.

6.7   Cross a spring-fed creek in the canyon bottom and immediately begin climbing out of the canyon.

Historic bridge beside Segment 3 - F. A. Barnes

6.8   Pass through a fence, and continue climbing the steep, overgrown, sandy, rocky, exposed south side of the canyon.

7.6 (11.8*)   Exit the first Cottonwood Canyon, rejoining the main gravel road. Beautiful Entrada formations are visible to the left of the road at the tip of Blue Chief Mesa. Continue climbing the switchbacks ahead.

10.9 (15.1*)   The climbing becomes less steep. Several mineral exploration roads are visible. However, riders should continue on what is obviously the main road. Line Canyon appears directly below the road on the left.

11.4 (15.6*)   Continue straight, through a "T" intersection.

12.0 (16.2*)   Begin a steeper descent as the trail surface becomes rocky with steps and pockets of sand. Sevenmile Canyon and the second Cottonwood Canyon will be visible ahead.

13.9 (18.1*) Enter the upper rimlands of the second Cottonwood Canyon. Stay right at a "T" intersection, heading toward the canyon.

14.8 (19.0*) Begin a very steep, rocky and technical descent along the side of the canyon. Most riders should walk here as a fall would be disastrous.

15.0 (19.2*) Bottom out and stop to peer into Cottonwood Canyon. Immediately begin climbing out of this depression.

15.9 (20.1*) At a "Y" intersection, stay right, keeping the cliff wall to the right and a large butte to the left. Continue climbing.

16.9 (21.1*) Hideout Canyon is visible to the left. The road surface is improving, becoming packed sediment.

17.6 (21.8*) Come to a car-sized rock and camping site at an intersection. Stay to the right and travel toward the Fisher Valley Ranch and the Onion Creek drainage.

18.0 (22.2*) At an intersection where this trail joins the Fisher Valley Ranch Road, Segment 3 ends.

Segment 3 - F. A. Barnes

47

Alternate Route:

5.4   Two roads coming in from the right within 100 feet of each other intersect the main gravel road. Stay left past both roads.

7.6   At an intersection, stay right. The left fork leads to Utah Bottoms and the Dolores River Ford, both of which are on private land.

9.6   Continue climbing on this steep ORV trail, as the Main Route comes in from the right. The canyon visible on the right is the first of the two Cottonwood Canyons. Rejoin the Main Route description. Mileages are indicated with an asterisk (*) for the Alternate Route.

OPTIONAL RIDING:

1. Dolores River Overlook Trail
2. Top of the World Trail
3. Power Pole Rim Trail
4. Utah Bottoms/Dolores River Ford Road
5. Slickrock above Dewey Bridge - 2.3 miles south of Utah 128.

Trails 1-3 are described in *Canyon Country* **Off-Road Vehicle Trails, Arches and La Sals Areas,** by F.A. Barnes.

The Utah Bottoms Road is reached at an intersection 7.5 miles from Dewey Bridge. At the "Y" intersection here, turn right if traveling in the Moab-Loma direction, left if going in the other direction.

The slickrock riding is not a trail, just a small playground.

F. A. Barnes

Entrada sandstone bluffs, Segment 3 - F. A. Barnes

Segment 3 - F. A. Barnes

SEGMENT 4
Dewey Bridge to Cisco Boat Landing

Distance: 20.6 Miles

Difficulty: Easy - 3; Moderate - 8.1; Difficult - 5; Awful - 4.5

Time: Main Route, 7 - 10 Hours; Alternate Route, 3-5 hours

Elevation: West - 4100 ft; High - 4800 ft; East - 4100 ft

Maps: **USGS** 7 1/2': Fisher Valley UT; Cisco or Mt. Wass 2 NE UT *
         BLM: Moab NE/4 1:100,000 metric
         Trails Illustrated: Moab Mountain Bike Routes **

* The USGS is revising maps of this area. Mt. Waas 2 NE is the name of the old map, which is difficult to find. Cisco is the name of the new map that is not in print at this time. There is also a Cisco 15' map, which only covers part of this area.

** The Trails Illustrated Map does not follow the route described here, between Dewey Bridge and McGraw Bottom. If following this map, do not look for BLM trail markers between Dewey Bridge and the McGraw Bottom highway crossing. After the highway crossing and on to the Cisco Boat Landing area, this map does follow the designated Moab-Loma Route (Kokopelli's Trail).

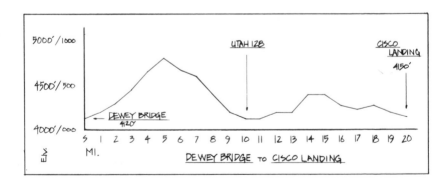

TRAIL SUMMARY:

The portion of this segment directly north of Dewey Bridge consists of 4.5 miles of very deep sand, so deep that a rider can barely travel downhill on a 30 degree slope. So deep that, except in early spring, it is not even challenging and must be walked in most places. Pushing a mountain bike through deep sand is the only task that comes to mind that is less enjoyable than hiking in knee-deep sand. Profuse cattle droppings in this area have also helped make travel along this stretch of trail unpleasant. Unfortunately, this miserable stretch passes some of the most beautiful Entrada sandstone bluffs in Utah! There are also several arches in the area. So, it is a trade off: sand, cow-pats and Entrada bluffs; or sanity and no Entrada bluffs. Both routes through this stretch of trail are described, so riders may choose.

The Main Route navigates the sand and encompasses the lovely Entrada formations above Yellow Jacket Canyon. In addition, the trail at the top of Yellow Jacket Canyon accesses some great slickrock riding. Bikers can take a side trip all the way to the tip of the Yellow Jacket Canyon formation where the view is spectacular. The trail between the top of the canyon and McGraw bottom is sandy and rocky. It is challenging but definitely ridable. There are, however, many side roads between the rim of Yellow Jacket Canyon and McGraw Bottom that are not on the maps. Most intersections are marked with BLM trail markers, though some are not.

The Alternate Route bypasses the sandy stretch by traveling north on Utah 128. This ride is also very scenic, following the Colorado River through McGraw Bottom. A variety of wildlife can often be seen along the river, including eagles and blue herons.

Beyond the point where the Main Route crosses Utah 128 and the Alternate Route turns off of Utah 128, the routes are the same. The majority of the trail is good gravel road or ORV trail. It also has a short stretch of easy singletrack. The terrain is somewhat hilly, high-desert terrain, with one portion skirting a bluff just above the Colorado River. The west end of the trail crosses the Colorado River on the original Dewey Bridge, an historic and beautiful suspension bridge that was an engineering marvel for its time. This bridge made it possible to travel from Moab to Grand Junction without having to ford the Colorado River.

This trail segment begins on the west end where Utah 128 crosses the Colorado River at Dewey Bridge. Park on the Moab side of the river, at the base of the old bridge, and begin the ride by crossing the river on the old bridge.

To access the east end of the segment, travel approximately 2.7 miles southeast out of Cisco, Utah, on the Pumphouse Road to an intersection marked "Fish Ford; Cisco Boat Landing." Follow the road to the left toward Cisco Landing. Cross a small bridge and at a "Y" intersection, stay left, NOT going to the boat landing. Continue a short distance to where a fence and cattleguard cross the road. Park in the large, flat area west of the fence and begin riding at the fence.

Historic view of Dewey Bridge - F. A. Barnes

MILEAGE LOG: WEST TO EAST

Main Route:

0.0   Cross the Colorado River on the old Dewey Bridge, cross Utah 128 and then pass through a large metal gate into a gravel pit area on private land. Be sure to close the gate. Use care to circumnavigate the gravel pit on the left, following the BLM trail markers, as heavy equipment sometimes operates in this area. Ascend a small saddle, leaving the gravel pit behind, and immediately encounter deep sand full of "excrement de bovine." Cattle can also be a hazard in this area. The grade steepens, and most riders will have to begin pushing their bikes at this point.

1.1   After climbing a steep hill with sandstone steps, pass through a fence and gate at the top of a rock ledge. Leave the gate as you find it. Continue slogging through the sand, following the BLM trail marker at the fence. Focus on the scenery, which is fantastic!

2.2   At a fork in the road, turn right onto a better defined road and continue climbing (probably on foot) through sand.

3.9   Enjoy the fantastic scenery, and don't forget to eat and drink, as sand-riding uses up lots of energy.

4.1   The trail forks. Follow the BLM marker to the right, still on very sandy trail.

4.4   Topping out on the Entrada rim above Yellow Jacket Canyon, look to the south for a beautiful panorama that includes Fisher Towers and the La Sals. At a fork in the road, go left.

4.6   At a "T" intersection, travel to the right and continue climbing. This is also the access point for the slickrock rim above Yellow Jacket Canyon. Don't ride through the potholes or cryptogamic soil!

4.7   Cross a stretch of slickrock. Follow the white-painted lines through this stretch. Ascend a steep hill.

5.0   After a steep hill-climb, intersect another road and follow the BLM trail marker uphill to the right.

MAP OF SEGMENT 4

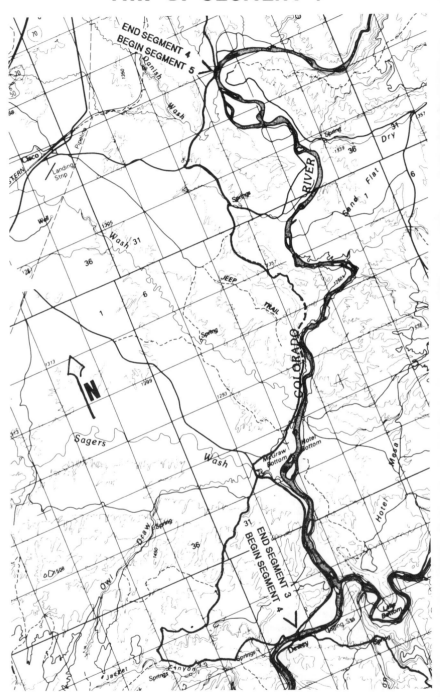

5.4 At another fork in the trail, follow the marker left.

5.8 Encounter a "Y" intersection and turn right to cross another large slab of slickrock.

6.1 Stay left at the BLM trail marker and ascend a sandy, rocky hill.

7.2 As the road forks, stay right. Travel up a hill and through a gate.

9.0 Go straight through this intersection as another road goes left. Begin descending.

9.5 Turn left onto the highway. Pass some corrals on the left and cross a bridge. Continue up the highway about 0.1 mile. There will be "UTAH 128" highway signs on both sides of the road.

9.6 Turn right onto a gravel road at the BLM trail marker that is attached to the "UTAH 128" sign. Ride toward a gravel pit area. The gravel road forks. Stay left and travel away from the gravel pit, up a hill.

11.2 (11.8*) At the "Y" intersection, turn left.

12.3 (12.9*) While traversing a cliff above the Colorado River, pass through a gate and descend a steep hill, bringing the route closer to the river as the road becomes a singletrack. The route is outlined with river-rock after it flattens out along the river.

13.5 (14.1*) The singletrack turns into an ORV road.

Reflections at beginning of Segment 4 F. A. Barnes

55

13.7 (14.3*) At an intersection, stay left and travel along the river bottom.

14.2 (14.8*) Go around the upper end of a slickrock arroyo and pass some shale bluffs. Begin climbing out of a steep drainage where cattle might be encountered. Beyond a small wash, stay left where another fork appears.

17.6 (18.2*) The ORV trail enters a gravel road. Turn left onto the gravel road and follow this road uphill to a sign saying, "Cisco Boat Landing; Fish Ford."

19.0 (19.6*) Turn right onto the road to Cisco Boat Landing. Go down a washboarded hill 1.7 miles, past the turn-off to Cisco Landing, to where the road passes through a fence. This trail segment ends here.

Arrowhead Arch - F. A. Barnes

Alternate Route:

0.0   Cross the old Dewey suspension bridge and turn right onto Utah 128. Ride 10.2 miles on the highway with the Colorado River on the right.

10.2   See a gravel pit on the right of the highway where two "UTAH 128" signs mark both sides of the road. Turn right onto a gravel road, as indicated by the BLM trail marker attached to the "UTAH 128" sign. Continue from here, using the description for the Main Route. Mileages are indicated with an asterisk (*) for the Alternate Route.

MILEAGE LOG: EAST TO WEST

0.0   Begin riding at the fence, just past the turn-off to the Cisco Boat Landing. On this graded gravel road, ride up a hill to where it intersects with the Pumphouse Road. This intersection is marked, "Fish Ford; Cisco Boat Landing."

1.7   Turn left toward Fish Ford and ride south toward the Colorado River.

3.0   Go around an "S" turn and watch for the BLM trail marker as the trail leaves the gravel road to the right. This intersection is difficult to see. Turn right on an ORV road and begin climbing a small hill to a salt flat where the road is smooth, packed sediment. In a few tenths of a mile, the road forks again. Stay left at a BLM trail marker and pass through a wash into a small valley. Watch for range cattle in this area.

6.4   Go around the head of an arroyo on slickrock and begin descending toward the Colorado River.

6.9   At an intersection, stay right along the river bottom. Climb a steep hill ending about 100 feet above the river.

8.3   Pass through a gate where the singletrack ends and an ORV trail begins. Descend toward Utah 128 and McGraw Bottom.

8.7   Cross through a fence where an old adobe structure is visible on the left.

9.4   At a "Y" intersection, stay right. The left fork goes to the gravel pit.

11.0   The ORV trail enters Utah 128. Turn left onto the highway and ride approximately 0.1 mile, across a bridge and past some corrals on the right. Exit the highway at an obvious pull-out just past the corrals. Begin climbing a steep, sandy, rocky hill. Riders wishing to avoid the deep sand north of Dewey Bridge should follow the Alternate Route.

Alternate Route:

11.0   Do not turn off of UTAH 128 at the corrals. Instead, continue riding on the highway for 10.2 miles. Just before the current Dewey Bridge, an old service station is visible on the left side of the road. Turn left at the station and cross the Colorado River on the old Dewey suspension bridge. This segment ends on the Moab side of the river.

Main Route, continued:

11.6   Another road comes in from the right. Go straight, continuing to climb on rocky, sandy ORV trail.

13.4   After a small descent, the road forks. Stay left and descend through a gate.

14.5   At a "Y" intersection, stay right as indicated by the BLM trail marker.

14.8   Having just crossed a slickrock slab, stay left at another intersection.

15.2   Top out a hill where a track comes in from the left. Stay right per the BLM marker and begin to see the Entrada formation above Yellow Jacket Canyon.

15.6   Make a 90 degree left turn onto a steep, rocky road and climb down over sandstone steps to another area of slickrock. Follow the white-painted lines across this slickrock playground, taking care not to ride through potholes or cryptogamic soil, or over plants.

15.9   Back on the dirt road, the amount of sand on the trail increases.

16.0   At an intersection, proceed left into a wash. There is also access here to the Entrada rim above Yellow Jacket Canyon for riders wishing to take a side trip.

16.2   After climbing out of a wash, stay right at an intersection.

16.5   Go left at another marked intersection. The trail surface is becoming more and more sandy.

18.4   At this intersection, turn left toward the beautiful red Entrada Bluffs. Riders MAY be able to ride for short distances here. Soon, however, the sand becomes too deep to ride. There may be cattle in this area. Keep your mind on the fantastic beauty of the canyon.

19.5   At the top of a hill, pass through a fence and walk down the steep sandstone. Watch out for cattle and fresh cow pies! Follow the cow path to the gravel pit. Ride around the outer edge of the gravel pit, following the BLM trail markers.

Views along Segment 4 - Peggy Utesch

20.5   At a large metal gate, proceed through and close the gate behind you. Turn left onto Utah 128 for a few hundred feet to the old service station. Turn right and cross the Colorado River on the old Dewey suspension bridge. This segment ends in the grassy parking area on the Moab side of the Colorado River.

OPTIONAL RIDING:

Entrada slickrock above Yellow Jacket Canyon.

Turn-off points as noted in the Mileage Logs.

Views along Segment 4 - Peggy Utesch

SEGMENT 5
Cisco Boat Landing to Rabbit Valley

Distance: 33.0 Miles

Difficulty: Easy - 23.5 Miles; Moderate - 19.5 Miles

Time: 3 - 5 Hours

Elevation: West - 4100 ft; High - 5000 ft; East 4600 ft

Maps: **USGS** 7 1/2': Big Triangle UT; Agate UT; Westwater UT/CO;
Bitter Creek Well UT/CO; Harley Dome UT
BLM: Moab NW/4 1:100,000 metric; Westwater UT/CO
1:100,000 metric; Grand Junction SW/4 1:100,000 metric

TRAIL SUMMARY:

This segment of the Moab-Loma Mountain Bike Route stays mostly on
graded gravel roads with a few stretches of ORV trail thrown in. The
route travels across grassy plateaus above the Colorado River, past two
beautiful sandstone monoliths called Castle Rocks, then travels along
McDonald Creek into Rabbit Valley. Although this is one of the longer
segments, much of it is on relatively flat terrain. The trail passes near
Ruby Canyon, which is a beautiful side trip for those wishing to hike. An
arroyo near the trail provides access to feeder canyons of Ruby Canyon.

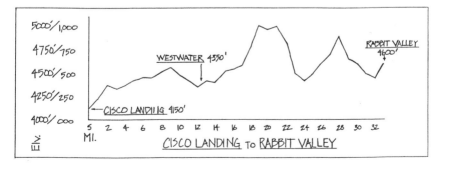

To access the west end of the trail, travel about 2.7 miles southeast out of Cisco, Utah, on the Pumphouse Road. Where this road intersects the road to Cisco Boat Landing, marked by a sign reading "Cisco Boat Landing; Fish Ford," head toward Cisco Boat Landing. Cross a small bridge and the road will "Y" in a mile or so. Stay left at that intersection, NOT taking the turn to Cisco Boat Landing. Shortly after this second intersection, come to a fence with a cattleguard. Park in the large flat area on the west side of the fence and begin riding at the fence.

The east access is reached by taking the Rabbit Valley Exit from I-70 in Colorado, near the Colorado/Utah border. Head south from the Interstate and park in a large, flat turnout along the road. Begin riding where an east-west gravel road meets the north/south Interstate access, making a "T" intersection. There is a BLM trail marker at this "T." Begin riding south at the intersection.

Peggy Utesch

MILEAGE LOG: WEST TO EAST

0.0   Begin riding east at a fence and cattleguard just beyond the Cisco Boat Landing turn-off.

0.1   Turn left off the gravel road onto a surface of packed sediment.

3.5   Stay right through a series of intersections, traveling parallel to the railroad tracks.

4.4   Several spur roads take off to the right and left. Stay on what is obviously the main road, parallel to the railroad.

5.8   Stay right and round a corner. The road surface is good and speeds of 20+mph can be reached.

7.4   Proceed straight through another series of intersections, continuing through the pristine grassland plains above Westwater Canyon.

9.9   Descend into a sandstone wash, and come to a large area of slickrock. Don't ride through the potholes or over the cryptogamic soil!

11.1   After descending a stretch of packed sediment, stay right as the road "Ys".

11.2   At another "Y", turn right.

12.5   Cross Westwater Creek and turn left onto a gravel road. Stay on the main gravel road for 4.0 miles watching for a Kokopelli's Trail marker.

16.5   At the Kokopelli's Trail marker, turn right onto a lesser road. Ascend across a large mesa, following additional trail markers.

MAP OF SEGMENT 5

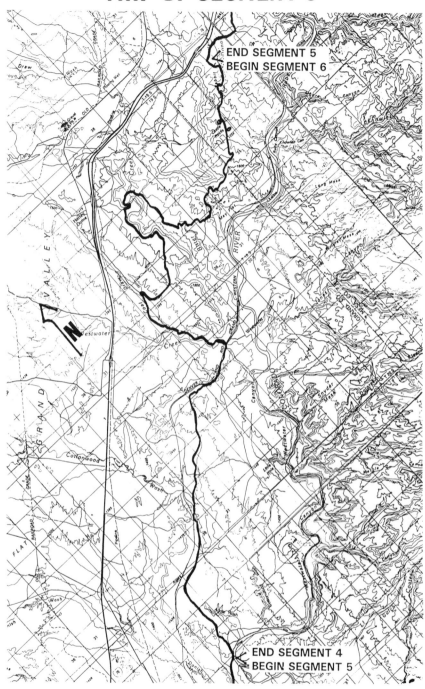

END SEGMENT 5
BEGIN SEGMENT 6

END SEGMENT 4
BEGIN SEGMENT 5

21.6   Turn right and travel 0.2 of a mile.

21.8   Turn left to descend into the Bitter Creek drainage.

26.0   Turn left and ride 3.9 miles to a junction.

29.9   Ruby Canyon is visible to the south. A feeder canyon near the
        road provides hiking access to side-canyons. As this is a BLM
        limited-use area, do not ride bikes off the road. Climb a hill and
        stay right at a fork in the road. Head toward two distinctive
        sandstone towers called Castle Rocks. The road surface is
        packed sediment with some sand.

31.1   Stay right at the intersection. Enter a small canyon through
        which McDonald Creek flows. Beware of flash floods in this
        area.

32.0   Stay right as a road comes in from the left, and exit the canyon.
        Note the beautiful pink sandstone formation to the right of the
        road.

32.4   Stay right at an intersection after exiting the canyon and crossing
        a small wash.

32.8   Stay left as the road forks.

33.0   This trail segment ends at the "T" intersection where the trail
        continues to the right. (Go straight through the intersection to
        access the Rabbit Valley exit from I-70.)

Peggy Utesch

MILEAGE LOG: EAST TO WEST

0.0   Begin riding south where the I-70 access intersects a road coming in from the left. There is a BLM trail marker at this intersection.

0.2   The road forks. Stay right at a sign noting public access. The road surface is sand and sediment.

0.6   At a fork in the road, travel left and cross a wash. Beautiful uplifts and pink/white sandstone formations are visible ahead.

1.0   Stay left, down a hill as the road forks. Enter a small canyon through which McDonald Creek flows when it is wet. A road comes in from the right. Continue left as the trail crisscrosses McDonald Creek. Although this creek is usually dry, beware of flash flood danger here.

1.9   Stay left as a lesser road comes in from the right while exiting the canyon.

2.3   Castle Rocks are visible ahead as the route gradually descends through pristine grasslands on an increasingly sandy road.

3.1   Turn right at a "Y" intersection, and follow the Kokopelli's Trail markers for 4.0 miles.

7.0   Turn right and drop into the Bitter Creek drainage.

8.1   Stay right at this intersection.

9.8   Stay right again.

10.5   Turn left and climb 400 feet to the rim of a high mesa.

11.2   Stay right and continue following the Kokopelli's Trail markers across the top of the mesa.

16.5   Turn left onto a gravel road - the Westwater access road - and travel 4.0 miles.

20.5   Intersect a major north/south gravel road coming in from I-70. Turn left onto this road, pass under the railroad bridge and turn right off the gravel road as the route crosses Westwater Creek. Watch for hawks and eagles in this area. (Turn right where the dirt road intersects the gravel road to access I-70. The left fork accesses the Westwater Ranger Station.)

21.8   At the "Y" intersection, stay left.

21.9   Stay left again, and begin climbing a stretch of packed sediment.

23.1   Cross a wash and climb onto a large area of slickrock. Respect the fragile ecosystems of the potholes and cryptogamic soil.

24.1   Top out the climb to a view of the La Sal mountains. The Castle Tower-Priest and Nuns formation is visible ahead. Begin descending over more stretches of slickrock.

Segment 5 - Peggy Utesch

25.6   Continue riding southwest through three small intersections.

27.2   Stay left around a corner and intersect a graded gravel road. Agate Wash is visible on the right. The road surface is good, and speeds of 20+mph can be reached.

28.6   Several spur roads exit the main route on the right and left. Stay on what is obviously the main road.

29.5   The trail turns south, away from the railroad. Stay left as several roads enter the main road from the right.

32.9   Intersect a gravel road that leads to the Cisco Boat Landing. Turn right onto this road.

33.0   Encounter a cattleguard at a fence where this segment ends.

OPTIONAL HIKING:

Feeder canyons of Ruby Canyon are enjoyable as wilderness hikes.

Colorado River, Segment 5 - Peggy Utesch

SEGMENT 6
Rabbit Valley to Loma

Distance: 19.5 Miles

Difficulty: Easy - 7; Moderate - 4; Difficult 8.5

Time: 6 - 8 Hours

Elevation: West - 4600 ft; High - 5,000 ft; East - 4400 ft

Maps: **USGS:** 7 1/2': Bitter Creek Well UT/CO; Ruby Canyon CO;
        Mack CO
        BLM: Westwater UT/CO & Grand Junction SW/4 1:100,000
        metric

TRAIL SUMMARY:

This final segment of the Moab-Loma Bike Route is definitely one of the most fun and challenging. For bikers who enjoy off-road riding, approximately 6 miles of this segment is exciting singletrack. In addition to climbing/descending one of the steepest grades on the whole system, the Rabbit Valley to Loma segment takes the rider across the maroon shale cliffs of the Morrison Formation, high above the Colorado River. The trail also fords Salt Creek, usually about 3 feet deep, although it can be deeper during spring run-off or after a heavy rain. The combination of spectacular scenery and challenging riding make this final trail segment one of the most rewarding.

Access to the west end of the trail is reached by exiting I-70 west of Grand Junction at Rabbit Valley. Head south from the Interstate and within 0.3 miles a wide turnout will be visible. Park there and continue south to where an east/west road comes in from the left. Begin riding at this intersection as indicated by the BLM trail marker.

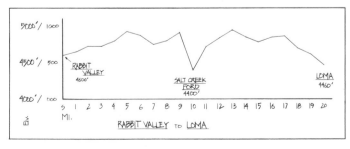

69

To reach the east end of the trail, exit I-70 at Loma. At an intersection south of the Interstate, head east - away from the Port of Entry. Travel down a short hill of broken pavement and around a turn to the Loma Boat Launch. Begin riding there.

MILEAGE LOG: WEST TO EAST

0.0   Begin riding where an east/west road intersects a north/south Interstate access road. A BLM marker designates this "T" intersection. Turn left and follow this graded gravel road for several miles, enjoying views of the Book Cliffs to the north. Travel through the hilly, sage-desert as the trail gradually climbs. The Interstate is visible from time to time on the left, as most of this route parallels I-70.

0.2   Cross a cattleguard at a fence and stay left.

0.8   Stay left per the BLM trail marker at a "Y" intersection.

1.7   Pass a stock-loading corral on the right of the road.

5.0   Intersect another main gravel road at the bottom of a hill. At the "Y" intersection, stay right as indicated by the trail marker. The left fork will travel under I-70 to the other side of the Interstate.

7.1   Turn left at an intersection. The road becomes a double-track dirt trail.

7.4   Turn right onto a stretch of singletrack which drops into the Salt Creek drainage. Within a tenth of a mile or so, the descent steepens as the trail surface becomes difficult with loose rock and sandy sediment. This is the steepest grade on the whole trail system.

8.1   At the bottom of the descent, pass through a willow infested flat to the edge of Salt Creek. The water is deeper on the west bank. Most riders will need to carry their bikes across this cold-water crossing. The exit on the far side is shallow. Use caution at this crossing if the water is high. Many animals also water in this area, so be respectful of their presence. Immediately begin a steep climb on more sandy, rocky singletrack. This entire stretch of singletrack is rated Difficult.

MAP OF SEGMENT 6

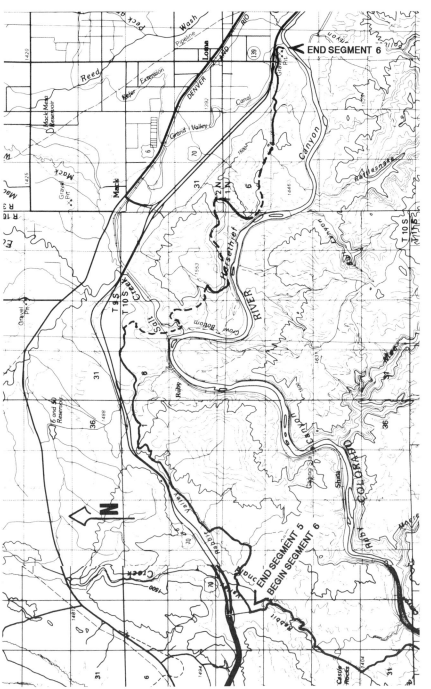

END SEGMENT 6

END SEGMENT 5
BEGIN SEGMENT 6

8.8   Top out of the climb, noting the railroad tunnel to the west and the Colorado River to the south.

9.0   Travel up an arroyo, follow the trail across patches of slickrock and watch for the cairns that mark the track.

10.3   This stretch of singletrack ends. Proceed on an off-road vehicle trail, staying left at several intersections marked with BLM trail signs.

11.0   Singletrack begins again and climbs through the steep, maroon shale slopes of the Morrison formation, high above the Colorado River. This stretch is again rated Difficult with a good deal of exposure.

12.7   Traverse along the edge of the sandstone cliffs above the Colorado. Follow the trail as it turns into an old off-road vehicle track which is mostly overgrown. Descend around a hillside to an intersection.

13.4   Intersect with a main gravel road just below a stock pond. The trail continues to the right, along the base of a sandstone uplift and climbs a low hill, through a saddle on a rocky road surface. This intersection has no trail marker -- perhaps vandalized as many markers have been. (Staying left on the gravel road, over a hill, accesses the frontage road leading to the Mack Exit from I-70.)

Segment 6 - Peggy Utesch

14.4   Singletrack begins again at a BLM trail marker and the trail is again rated Difficult. Horsethief Canyon and the Colorado River are visible below the trail.

15.3   Still traversing sandstone cliffs above the river, pass through a fence and gate and above the first of five side-canyons, still on singletrack.

15.6   The singletrack ends and ORV trail begins.

16.4   At an intersection, go left and continue along the canyon rim.

16.8   Stay left at another intersection as indicated by the trail marker. Travel away from the river cliffs.

17.3   Descend a steep, rocky hill.

17.9   Still traveling on ORV trail, intersect a main gravel road and turn left.

18.3   Stay right at this junction. Follow this dirt road back to the Interstate access intersection. The Port of Entry is visible on the left. At the Interstate intersection, turn right, travel down a hill on a surface of broken pavement and gravel, to the parking lot for the Loma Boat Launch. This route segment and the Moab-Loma Mountain Bike Route end here.

MILEAGE LOG: EAST TO WEST

0.0   Begin riding at the Loma Boat Launch parking lot. Travel up a hill of broken pavement to the intersection of the Interstate exit, the road leading to the Port of Entry, and a dirt road. Stay left on the dirt road.

1.2   The dirt road forks. Travel left and climb a switchback through a notch. From the top of the hill, Horsethief Canyon is visible, as well as some tower formations in the distance.

1.6   At another fork in the road, take the more primitive track to the right. The trail surface becomes powdered red sediment.

2.1   Begin climbing a steep, rocky hill.

2.7   Stay right at this junction, as the trail descends to the canyon rim above the Colorado River and winds along the heads of several feeder canyons.

3.1   Stay right at a fork in the trail.

3.9   The first singletrack stretch begins. The track is marked with stones and cairns along the way.

4.2   Round the head of the fifth side-canyon. Pass through a fence and gate and continue on singletrack, rated Difficult.

5.1   Traveling along the Colorado River above Horsethief Canyon,

6.1   What appears to be a cow path takes off to the left, just below a stock pond, and climbs around a steep sandy hill to the south. Follow this trail. (The gravel road to the right which climbs a steep, sandy hill to a fence and down the other side is the access to Mack Exit from I-70. The return route to Loma is known as "Mary's Loop.")

8.5   The singletrack ends as the trail becomes an ORV trail.

9.2   Singletrack begins again.

Segment 6 - Peggy Utesch

10.4   The trail dips into an arroyo and climbs out again. Follow the cairns across the slickrock.

10.7   The Salt Creek drainage and railroad tunnel are visible ahead. Descend a steep, sandy hill into the creek bottom. Many animals drink here, so be respectful of their presence.

11.3   Ford Salt Creek. The entrance to the water from this direction is shallow. Usually the water is about 3' deep at the exit, although this can vary depending on spring run-off or rain. Carry bikes across the creek and climb out at the steep bank-cut on the far side. Use caution at this crossing when the water is high. Once across the creek, cross a sandy, willow-infested flat to the bottom of a steep, sandy hill and begin ascending the steepest grade on the trail system.

12.1   Top out the climb to a beautiful view in all directions. The Book Cliffs are visible to the north, with the Colorado River canyon to the south. Intersect a road and stay left, heading west.

12.4   The ORV road enters a main gravel road. Go right on this road as it dips and climbs through beautiful high desert and small canyons. The Interstate is visible to the right from time to time.

14.5   Intersect another main gravel road at the bottom of a hill ahead. Turn left, as indicated by the trail marker. The right fork travels under I-70 to the other side of the Interstate.

17.8   Still on gravel road, pass some stock pens visible on the left. Several lesser roads also intersect this road. Stay on the main route.

18.7   Stay right, per the BLM trail marker, at an intersection.

19.3   Cross a cattleguard at a fence and stay right as the road forks.

19.5   After passing a bluff on the right, intersect a north/south road. This segment ends at this intersection, marked by a BLM trail marker. Turn left to continue on Segment 5, or access I-70 by staying right (north).

OPTIONAL RIDING:

1. Mary's Loop. From Loma, ride the Moab-Loma Route to Mile 6.1. Leave the described route and travel over a low hill to a frontage road near the Mack Exit of I-70. Continue back to Loma on the frontage road. The whole loop is about 13 miles.

2. There are many small roads spurring from the main route all along this segment. All simply take a slightly different route and rejoin the main route within 1/2 mile.

3. If bikers wish to shorten this ride, the trail can be accessed at the Mack Exit from I-70. This alternate starting/ending point shortens the ride by about six miles.

Views along Segment 6 - Peggy Utesch

AUTHOR'S FAVORITE RIDES

Selecting a favorite segment of the Moab-Loma Route (Kokopelli's Trail) is difficult! Each segment is so completely different, having a magical quality all its own. I will always remember a beautiful October evening near Rill Creek in Segment 1. The coyotes chattered into the night as a breeze, warm with the last heat of summer, danced through the smoke of our campfire. Several meteorites streaked across the Milky Way, and we dreamed of being able to spend every night in such peaceful solitude.

When riding Segment 3, those enchanting desert dwellers, the collared lizards, played with us. Around each corner, these colorful sunbathers scurried out of the trail. The exhilarating challenge of navigating the two Cottonwood Canyons, each with its unique sandstone formations and hidden secrets, also made Segment 3 memorable.

Each day and each unique place in the desert presents gifts and challenges of its own. The desert is a special place with the ubiquitous susurration of years-gone-by carved into the landscape by the winds and waters of time.

In one sense, the whole region is my favorite ride.

Peggy Utesch

Photo by Charles Palek

ACKNOWLEDGMENTS

I would like to express thanks to several special people who made this book possible:

Fran Barnes - for inspiring me, teaching me and being
patient with me as I learned from him some of
the intricacies of writing and publishing.

Bob Utesch - whose help with the field work, love of maps
and fastidious attention to detail helped me remain rational
through the process of researching and writing my first book.

Russ Von Koch - for verifying and sharing information about the
the BLM's current and future recreation plans.

Fred Barta of Latent Image Photography for allowing
me to use his darkroom facilities.

Jean Gonzales - for understanding
and for buying me Margaritas
when I needed them most.

But most of all to my parents,
Vern and Shirley Adams,
who taught me to love adventure.

F. A. Barnes

BIBLIOGRAPHY

THIRST, by B. J. Rolls and E. T. Rolls. University of Oxford Department of Experimental Psychology, Oxford, England. Cambridge University Press, 1982.

ESSAYS ON TEMPERATURE REGULATION, edited by J. Bligh and R. More. North-Holland Publishing Company, 1972.

THE PSYCHOLOGY OF EATING AND DRINKING, by A. W. Logue. W. H. Freeman and Company, NY, 1986.

EXERCISE PHYSIOLOGY: ENERGY, NUTRITION AND HUMAN PERFORMANCE, by William D. McArdle, Frank I. Katch, Victor L. Katch. Lea & Febinger, Philadelphia, 1981.

GREG LEMOND'S COMPLETE BOOK OF BICYCLING, by Greg LeMond and Kent Gordes. Putnam Publishing Group, NY, 1988.

EAT TO WIN, The Sports Nutrition Bible, by Robert Haas. Rawson Associates, NY, 1983.

HOW TO S— IN THE WOODS, by Kathleen Meyer. 10 (Ten) Speed Press, Berkeley, CA, 1989.

Sand Flats, Segment 1 - F. A. Barnes

FURTHER READING

Those who wish to know more about the unique and fascinating canyon country of southeastern Utah will find other books and maps in the *Canyon Country* series both useful and informative. They are stocked by many visitor centers and retail outlets in the region.

The listed books are profusely illustrated with photographs, charts, graphs, maps and original artwork. The maps are also illustrated with representative photographs.

GENERAL INFORMATION

Canyon Country HIGHWAY TOURING by F. A. Barnes. A guide to the highways and roads in the region that can safely be traveled by highway vehicles, plus descriptions of all the national and state parks and monuments and other special areas in the region.

Canyon Country EXPLORING by F. A. Barnes. A brief history of early explorations plus details concerning the administration of this vast area of public land and exploring the region today by land, air and water.

Canyon Country CAMPING by F. A. Barnes. A complete guide to all kinds of camping in the region, including highway pull-offs, developed public and commercial campgrounds and backcountry camping from vehicles and backpacks.

Canyon Country GEOLOGY by F. A. Barnes. A summary of the unique geologic history of the region for the general reader, with a list of its unusual land-forms and a section on rock collecting.

Canyon Country PREHISTORIC INDIANS by Barnes & Pendleton. A detailed description of the region's two major prehistoric Indian cultures, with sections telling where to view their ruins, rock art and artifacts.

Canyon Country PREHISTORIC ROCK ART by F. A. Barnes. A comprehensive study of the mysterious prehistoric rock art found throughout the region, with a section listing places where it can be viewed.

Canyon Country ARCHES & BRIDGES by F. A. Barnes. A complete description of the unique natural arches, bridges and windows found throughout the region, with hundreds depicted.

UTAH CANYON COUNTRY by F. A. Barnes. An overview of the entire region's natural and human history, parks and monuments, and recreational opportunities, illustrated in full color.

CANYONLANDS NATIONAL PARK - *Early History & First Descriptions* by F. A. Barnes. A summary of the early history of this uniquely spectacular national park including quotes from the journals of the first explorers to see and describe it.

Canyon Country's CANYON RIMS RECREATION AREA by F. A. and M. M. Barnes. A description of the natural and human history and outstanding scenic beauty in this immense area to the east of Canyonlands National Park, plus a summary of its outstanding recreational opportunities.